'SEE MY
UP-TIPP
THE SECRET OF
MY HUMAN
HEART...'

JACK KEROUAC
Born 1922, Lowell, Massachusetts, USA
Died 1969, St. Petersburg, Florida, USA

These two journal entries about Jack Kerouac's itinerant experiences in the United States were first published in *Lonesome Traveler*, in 1960.

KEROUAC IN PENGUIN MODERN CLASSICS

**JACK KEROUAC**

*Piers of the Homeless Night*

PENGUIN BOOKS

PENGUIN CLASSICS

UK | USA | Canada | Ireland | Australia
India | New Zealand | South Africa

Penguin Books is part of the Penguin Random House group
of companies whose addresses can be found at
global.penguinrandomhouse.com.

Penguin
Random House
UK

This selection first published 2018
001

Set in 12/15 pt Dante MT Std
Typeset by Jouve (UK), Milton Keynes
Printed in Great Britain by Clays Ltd, St Ives plc

ISBN: 978–0–241–33918–3

www.greenpenguin.co.uk

MIX
Paper from
responsible sources
FSC® C018179

Penguin Random House is committed to a
sustainable future for our business, our readers
and our planet. This book is made from Forest
Stewardship Council® certified paper.

# Contents

*Piers of the Homeless Night*


HERE DOWN ON DARK EARTH
     before we all go to Heaven
VISIONS OF AMERICA
All that hitchhikin
All that railroadin
All that comin back
     to America
Via Mexican & Canadian borders . . .

   Less begin with the sight of me with collar huddled
up close to neck and tied around with a handkerchief
to keep it tight and snug, as I go trudging across the
bleak, dark warehouse lots of the ever lovin San
Pedro waterfront, the oil refineries smelling in the
damp foggish night of Christmas 1951 just like burning rubber and the brought-up mysteries of Sea
Hag Pacific, where just off to my left as I trudge you
can see the oily skeel of old bay waters marching

up to hug the scumming posts and out on over the flatiron waters are the lights ululating in the moving tide and also lights of ships and bum boats themselves moving and closing in and leaving this last lip of American land. – Out on that dark ocean, that wild dark sea, where the worm invisibly rides to come, like a hag flying and laid out as if casually on sad sofa but her hair flying and she's on her way to find the crimson joy of lovers and eat it up, Death by name, the doom and death ship the SS *Roamer*, painted black with orange booms, was coming now like a ghost and without a sound except for its vastly shuddering engine, to be warped & wailed in at the Pedro pier, fresh from a run from New York through the Panamy canal, and aboard's my old buddy Deni Bleu let's call him who had me travel 3,000 miles overland on buses, with the promise he will get me on and I sail the rest of the trip around the world. – And since I'm well and on the bum again & aint got nothing else to do, but roam, long-faced, the real America, with my unreal heart, here I am eager and ready to be a big busted nose scullion or dishwasher on the old scoff scow s'long as I can buy my next fancy shirt in a Hong Kong haberdashery or wave a polo mallet in some old Singapore bar or play the horses in Australian, it's all the same to me as long as it can be exciting and goes around the world.

For weeks I have been traveling on the road, west from New York, and waiting up in Frisco at a friend's house meanwhile earning an extra 50 bucks working the Christmas rush as a baggagehandler with the old sop out railroad, have just now come the 500 miles down from Frisco as an honored secret guest in the caboose of the Zipper first class freight train thanx to my connections on the railroad up there and now I think I'm going to be a big seaman, I'll get on the *Roamer* right here in Pedro, so I think fondly, anyway if it wasnt for this shipping I'd sure like it maybe to be a railroad man, learn to be a brakeman, and get paid to ride that old zooming Zipper. – But I'd been sick, a sudden choking awful cold of the virus X type California style, and could hardly see out the dusty window of the caboose as it flashed past the snowy breaking surf at Surf and Tangair and Gaviota on the division that runs that moony rail between San Luis Obispo and Santa Barbara. – I'd tried my best to appreciate a good ride but could only lay flat on the caboose seat with my face buried in my bundled jacket and every conductor from San Jose to Los Angeles had had to wake me up to ask me about my qualifications, I was a brakeman's brother and a brakeman in Texas Division myself, so whenever I looked up thinking 'Ole Jack you are now actually riding in a caboose and going along the surf on the spectrallest railroad you'd ever in your wildest dreams wanta ride, like a kid's dream, why is it you cant lift your head and look out there and appreciate the feathery shore of California the last land being feathered by fine powdery skeel of doorstop sills of doorstep water weaving in from every Orient and bay boom shroud from here to Catteras Flapperas Voldivious and Gratteras, boy,' but I'd raise my head, and nothing there was to see, except my bloodshot soul, and vague hints of unreal moon shinin on an unreal sea, and the flashby quick of the pebbles of the road bed, the rail in the starlight. – Arriving in LA in the morning and I stagger with full huge cuddlebag on shoulder from the LA yards clear into downtown Main Street LA where I laid up in a hotel room 24 hours drinking bourbon lemon juice and anacin and seeing as I lay on my back a vision of America that had no end – which was only beginning – thinking, tho, 'I'll get on the *Roamer* at Pedro and be gone for Japan before you can say boo.' – Looking out the window when I felt a little better and digging the hot sunny streets of LA Christmas, going down finally to the skid row poolhalls and shoe shine joints and gouging around, waiting for the time when the *Roamer* would warp in at the Pedro pier, where I was to meet Deni right at the gangplank with the gun he'd sent ahead.

More reasons than one for the meeting in Pedro – he'd sent a gun ahead inside of a book which he'd carefully cut and hollowed out and made into a tight neat package covered with brown paper and tied with string, addressed to a girl in Hollywood, Helen something, with address which he gave me, 'Now Kerouac when you get to Hollywood you go immediately to Helen's and ask her for that package I sent her, then you carefully open it in your hotel room and there's the gun and it's loaded so be careful dont shoot your finger off, then you put it in your pocket, do you hear me Kerouac, has it gotten into your heskefuffle frantic imagination – but now you've got a little errand to do for me, for your boy Denny Blue, remember we went to school together, we thought up ways to survive together to scrounge for pennies we were even cops together we even married the same woman,' (cough) 'I mean, – we both wanted the same woman, Kerouac, it's up to you now now to help defend me against the evil of Matthew Peters, you bring that gun with you' poking me and emphatically pronouncing each word, and poking me with each word 'and bring it on you and dont get caught and dont miss the boat whatever you do.' – A plan so absurd, so typical of this maniac, I came of course without the gun, without even looking up Helen, but just in my beatup jacket hurrying, almost late, I could see her masts close in against the pier, night, spotlights everywhere, down that dismal long plaza of refineries and oil storage tanks, on my poor scuffledown shoes that had begun a real journey now – starting in New York to follow the fool ship but it was about to be made plain to me in the first 24 hours I'd never get on no ship – didnt know it then, but was doomed to stay in America, always, road rail or waterscrew, it'll always be America (Orient-bound ships chugging up the Mississippi, as will be shown later.) – No gun, huddled against the awful winter damp of Pedro and Long Beach, in the night, passing the Puss n' Boots factory on a corner with little lawn out front and American flagpoles and a big tuna fish ad inside the same building they make fish for humans and for cats – passing the Matson piers, the Lurline not in. – Eyes peeled for Matthew Peters the villain who was behind the need for the gun.

It went back, maniacally, to further earlier events in this gnashing huge movie of earth only a piece of which here's offered by me, long tho it is, how wild can the world be until finally you realize 'O well it's just repetitious anyway.' – But Deni had deliberately wrecked this Matthew Peters' car. It seems they had lived together and with a bunch of girls in Hollywood. They were seamen. You saw snapshots of them sitting around sunny pools in bathingsuits and with blondes and in big hugging poses. Deni tall, fattish, dark, smiling white teeth hypocrite's smile, Matthew Peters an extremely handsome blond with a self-assured grim expression or (morbid) expression of sin and silence, the hero – of the group, of the time – so that you hear it always spoken behind the hand, the confidential stories told to you by every drunk and non-drunk in every bar and non-bar from here to the other side of all the Tathagata worlds in the 10 Quarters of the universe, it's like the ghosts of all the mosquitos that had ever lived, the density of the story of the world all of it would be enough to drown the Pacific as many times as you could remove a grain of sand from its sandy bed. The big story was, the big complaint, that I heard chanted, from Deni, an old complainer and chanter and one of the most vituperative of complainers, 'While I was scrounging around in the garbage cans and barrels of Hollywood mind you, going behind those very fancy apartment houses and at night, late, very quietly sneaking around, getting bottles for 5 cent deposits and putting them in my little bag, for extra money, when we couldnt get longshore work and nor get a ship for love nor money, Matthew, with his airy ways, was having big parties and spending every cent he could get from my grimy hands and not once, N O TTT Once, did I hear one W O R D of appreciation – you can imagine how I felt when finally he took my best girl and took off with her for a night – I sneaked to his garage where he had his car parked, I very quietly backed it out without starting the motor, I let it roll down the street, and then man I was on my way to Frisco, drinking beer from cans

– I could tell you a story –' and so he goes on with his story, told in his own inimitable way, how he wrecked the car in Cucamonga California, a head-on crash into some tree, how he almost got killed, how the cops were, and lawyers, and papers, and troubles, and how he finally got to Frisco, and got another ship, and how Matthew Peters who knew he was on the *Roamer*, would be waiting at the pierhead this very same clammy cold night in Pedro with a gun, a knife, henchmen, friends, anything and everything. – Deni was going to step off the ship looking in all directions, ready to throw himself flat on the ground, and I was to be waiting there at the foot of the gangplank and hand him the gun real quick – all in the foggy foggy night –

'Alright tell me a story.'

'Gently now.'

'Well you're the one who started all this.'

'Gently, gently' says Deni in his own peculiar way saying 'JHENT' very loud with mouth moawed like a radio announcer to pronounce every sound and then the 'LY' is just said English-wise, it was a trick we'd both picked up at a certain madcap prep school where everybody went around talking like very high smotche smahz, . . . now shmuz, SHmazaa zzz, inexplicable the foolish tricks of schoolboys long ago, lost, – which Deni now in the absurd San Pedro night was still quipping up to fogs, as if it didnt make any difference. – 'GENT ly' says Deni taking a firm grip on my arm and holding me tight and looking at me seriously, he's about six-three and he's looking down at little five-nine me and his eyes are dark, glitlering, you can see he's mad, you can see his conception of life is something no one else has ever had and ever will have tho just as seriously he can go around believing and claiming his theory about me for instance, 'Kerouac is a victim, a VIC timm of his own i ma JHI NA Tion.' – Or his favorite joke about me, which is supposed to be so funny and is the saddest story he ever told or anyone ever told, 'Kerouac wouldnt accept a leg of fried chicken one night and when I asked him why he'd said "Im thinking about the poor starving people of Europe" . . . Hyaa WA W W W' and he goes off on his fantastic laugh which is a great shrieking lofter into a sky designed specially for him and which I always see over him when I think of him, the black night, the around the world night, the night he stood on the pier in

Honolulu with contraband Japanese kimonos on, four of them, and the customs guards made him undress down to em and there he stands at night on the platform in Japanese kimonos, big huge Deni Bleu, downcast & very very unhappy – 'I could tell you a story that's so long I couldnt finish telling it to you if we took a trip around the world, Kerouac, you but you dont you wont you never listen – Kerouac what WHAT are you going to tell the poor people starving in Europe about the Puss n' Boots plant there with the tuna fish in back, H MHmmh Ya a YYaawww Yawww, *they make the same food for cats and people*, Yyorr yhOOOOOOOOOO!' – And when he laughed like that you know he was having a hell of a good time and lonely in it, because I never saw it to fail, the fellas on the ship and all ships he ever sailed on couldnt see what was so funny what with all, also, his practical joking, which I'll show. – 'I wrecked Matthew Peters' car you understand – now let me say of course I didnt do it deliberately, Matthew Peters would like to think so, a lot of evil skulls like to believe so, Paul Lyman likes to believe so he can also believe I stole his wife which I assure you Kerouac I ding e do, it was my buddy Harry

McKinley who stole Paul Lyman's wife – I drove Matthew's car to Frisco, I was going to leave it there on the street and ship out, he would have got the thing back but unfortunately, Kerouac, life isnt always outcome could coming the way we like and tie but the name of the town I can never and I shall never be able to – there, up, er, Kerouac, you're not listening,' gripping my arm, 'Gently now, are you listening to what I'm SAYING to you!'

'Of course I'm listening.'

'Then why are you going myu, m, hu, what's up there, the birds up there, you heard the bird up there, mmmmy' turning away with a little shnuffle lonely laugh, this is when I see the true Deni, now, when he turns away, it isnt a big joke, there was no way to make it a big joke, he was talking to me and then he tried to make a joke out of my seeming not-listening and it wasnt funny because I was listening, in fact I was seriously listening as always to all his complaints and songs and but he turned away and had tried and in a forlorn little look into his own, as if, past, you see the double chin or dimplechin of some big baby nature folding up and with rue, with a heartbreaking, French giving-up, humility, meekness even, he ran the gamut from absolutely malicious plotting and scheming and practical joking, to big angel Ananda baby mourning in the night, I saw him I know. – 'Cucamonga, Practamonga, Calamongonata, I shall never remember the name of that town, but I ran the car head-on into a tree, Jack, and that was that and I was set upon by every scroungy cop lawyer judge doctor indian chief insurance salesman conman type in the – I tell you I was lucky to get away alive I had to wire home for all kinds of money, as you know my mother in Vermont has all my savings and when I'm in a real pitch I always wire home, it's my money.'

'Yes Deni.' But to cap everything there was Matthew Peters' buddy Paul Lyman, who had a wife, who ran away with Harry McKinley or in some way that I could never understand, they took a lot of money and got on an Orient bound passenger vessel and were now living with an alcoholic major in a villa in Singapore and having a big time in white duck trousers and tennis shoes but Lyman the husband, also a seaman and in fact a shipmate of Matthew Peters' and (tho Den didnt know at this time, aboard the Lurline both of them) (keep that) bang, he was convinced Deni was behind that too, and so the both of them had sworn to kill Deni or get Deni and according to Deni they were going to be on the pier when the ship came in that night, with guns and friends, and I was to be there, ready, when Deni comes off the gangplank swiftly and all dressed up to go to Hollywood to see his stars and girls and all the big things he'd written me I'm to step up quickly and hand him the gun, loaded and cocked, and Deni, looking around carefully to see no shadows leap up, ready to throw himself flat on the ground, takes the gun from me and together we cut into the darkness of the waterfront and rush to town – for further events, developments –

So now the *Roamer* was coming in, it was being straightened out along the concrete pier, I stood and spoke quietly to one of the after deckhands struggling with ropes, 'Where's the carpenter?'

'Who Blue? the – I'll see him in a minute.' A few other requests and out comes Deni just as the ship is being winched and secured and the ordinary's putting out the rat guards and the captain's blowed his little whistle and that incomprehensible slow huge slowmotion eternity move of ships is done, you hear the churns the backwater churns, the pissing of scuppers – the big ghostly trip is done, the ship is in – the same human faces are on the deck – and here comes Deni in his dungarees and unbelievably in the foggy night he sees his boy standing right there on the quai, just as planned, with hands-a-pockets, almost could reach out and touch him.

'There you are Kerouac, I never thought you'd be here.'

'You told me to, didn't you –'

'Wait, another half hour to finish up and clean up and dress, I'll be right with you – anybody around?'

'I dont know.' I looked around. I have been looking around for a half hour, at parked cars, dark corners, holes of sheds, door holes, niches, crypts of Egypt, waterfront rat holes, crapule doorholes, and beercan clouts, midmast booms and fishing eagles – bah, nowhere, the heroes were nowhere to be seen.

Two of the saddest dogs you ever saw (haw haw haw) walking off that pier, in the dark, past a few customs guards who gave Deni a customary little look and wouldnt have found the gun in his pocket anyway but he'd taken all those pains to mail it in that hollowed-out tome and now as we peered around together he whispered 'Well have you got it?'

'Yea yea in my pocket.'

'Hang on to it, give to me outside on the street.'

'Dont worry.'

'I guess they're not here, but you never can tell.'

'I looked everywhere.'

'We'll get outa here and make tracks – I've got it all planned Kerouac what we're gonna do tonight tomorrow and the whole weekend; I've been talking to all the cooks, we've got it all planned, a letter for you down to Jim Jackson at the hall and you're going to sleep in the cadets' stateroom on board, think of it Kerouac a whole stateroom to yourself, and Mr Smith has agreed to come with us and celebrate, hm a mahya.' – Mr Smith was the fat pale potbellied wizard of the bottom skeels of the engine room, a wiper or oiler or general watertender, he was the funniest old guy you'd ever wish to see and already Deni was laughing and feeling good and forgetting the imaginary enemies – out on the pier street it was evident we were in the clear. Deni was wearing an expensive Hong Kong blue serge suit, with soldiers in his shoulder pads and a fine drape, a beautiful suit, in which, now, beside mine in my road rags, he stomped along like a French farmer throwing his biggest brogans over the rows *de bledeine*, like a Boston hoodlum scuffling along the Common on Saturday night to see the guys at the poolhall but in his own way, with cherubic Deni smile that was heightened tonight by the fog making his face jovial round and red, tho not old, but what with the sunshine of the trip thru the canal he looked like a Dickens character stepping to his post chaise and dusty roads, only what a dismal scene spread before us as we walked. – Always with Deni it's walking, long long walks, he wouldnt spend a dollar on a cab because he likes to walk but also there were those days when he went out with my first wife and used to shove her right through the subway turnstile before she could realize what happened, from the back naturally – a charming little trick – to save a nickel – a pastime at which old Den's unbeatable, as could be shown. – We came to the Pacific Red Car tracks after a fast hike of about 20 minutes along those dreary refineries and waterskeel slaphouse stop holes, under impossible skies laden I suppose with stars but you could just see their dirty blur in the Southern Californian

Christmas – 'Kerouac we are now at the Pacific Red Car tracks, do you have any faint idea as to what that thing is can you tell that you think you can, but Kerouac you have always struck me as being the funniest man I have ever known . . .'

'No, Deni YOU are the funniest man I ever known –'

'Dont interrupt, dont drool, dont –' the way he answered and always talked and he's leading the way across the Red Car tracks, to a hotel, in downtown long Pedro where someone was supposed to meet us with blondes and so he bought enroute a couple of small hand cases of beer for us to portable around with, and when we got to the hotel, which had potted palms and potted barfronts and cars parked, and everything dead and windless with that dead California sad windless smoke-smog, and the Pachucos going by in a hot rod and Deni says 'You see that bunch of Mexicans in that car with their blue jeans, they got one of our seamen here last Christmas, about a year ago today, he was doing nothing but minding his own business, but they jumped right out that car and beat the living hell out of him – they take his money – no money, it's just to be mean, they're Pachucos, they just like to beat up on people for the hell of it –'

'When I was in Mexico it didnt seem to me the Mexicans there were like that –'

'The Mexicans in the US is another matter Kerouac, if you'd been around the world like I have you could see as I do a few of the rough facts of life that apparently with you and the poor people starving in Europe you'll never NEVER under STAAANNND . . .' gripping my arm again, swinging as he walks, like in our prep school days when we used to go up the sunny morning hill, to Horace Mann, at 246th in Manhattan, on the rock cliffs over by the Van Cortlandt park, the little road, going up thru English halftimber cottages and apartment houses, to the ivied school on top, the whole bunch swinging uphill to school but nobody ever went as fast as Deni as he never paused to take a breath, the climb was very sharp, most had to wind and work and whine and moan along but Deni swung it with his big glad laugh. – In those days he'd sell daggers to the rich little fourth formers, in back of the toilets. – He was up to more tricks tonight – 'Kerouac I'm going to introduce you to two cucamongas in

Hollywood tonight if we can get there on time, tomorrow for sure . . . two cucamongas living in a house, in an apartment house, the whole thing built clear around a swimmingpool, do you understand what I said, Kerouac? . . . a swimmingpool, that you go swimming in –'

'I know, I know, I seen it in that picture of you and Matthew Peters and all the blondes, great . . . What we do, work on em?'

'Wait, a minute before I explain the rest of the story to you, hand me the gun.'

'I havent got the gun you fool, I was only saying that so you'd get off the ship . . . I was ready to help you if anything happened.'

'YOU HAVENT GOT IT?' It dawned on him he had boasted to the whole crew 'My boy's out there on the pier with the gun, what did I tell ya' and he had earlier, when the ship left New York, posted a big absurd typically Deni ridiculous poster printed in red ink on a piece of paper, 'WARNING, THERE ARE FELLOWS ON THE WEST COAST BY THE NAMES OF MATTHEW PETERS AND PAUL LYMAN WOULD LIKE NOTHING BETTER THAN TO CLOBBER THE CAR-PENTER OF THE ROAMER DENI E. BLEU IF ONLY

THEY COULD BUT ANY SHIPMATES OF THE BLEU
WANT TO HELP BE ON THE LOOKOUT FOR THOSE
TWO EVIL SCROUNGERS WHEN THE SHIP PUTS IN AT
PEDRO AND THERE WILL BE APPRECIATION SIGNED
CARPT. FREE DRINKS IN THE CARPT. TONIGHT' – and
then by word in the messroom he'd loudly boasted
his boy.

'I knew you'd tell everyone I had the gun, so I said
I did. Didnt you feel better walking off the ship?'

'Where is it?'

'I didnt even go.'

'Then it's still there. We'll have to pick it up
tonight.' He was lost in thought – it was okay.

Deni had big plans for what was going to happen
at the hotel, which was the El Carrido Per to Mot-
paotta California potator hotel as I say with potted
palmettos and seamen inside and also hotrod cham-
pion sons of aircraft computators of Long Beach, the
whole general and really dismal California culture
a palpable hangout for it, where you saw the dim
interiors where you saw the Hawaiian shirted and
be-wristwatched, tanned strong young men tilting
long thin beers to their mouths and leaning and
mincing with broads in fancy necklaces and with

little white ivory things at their tanned ears and a whole blank blue in their eyes that you saw, also a bestial cruelty hidden and the smell of beer and smoke and smart smell of the cool inside plush cocktail lounge all that Americanness that in my youth had me get wild to be in it and leave my home and go off be big hero in the American romance-me-jazz night. – That had made Deni lose his head too, at one time he had been a sad infuriated French boy brought over on a ship to attend American private schools at which time hate smoldered in his bones and in his dark eyes and he wanted to kill the world – but a little of the Sage and Wisdom education from the Masters of the High West and he wanted to do his hating and killing in cocktail lounges learned from Franchot Tone movies and God knows where and what else. – We come up to this thing down the drear boulevard, phantasm street with its very bright street lamps and very bright but somber palms jutting out of the sidewalk all pineapple-ribbed and rising into the indefinable California night sky and no wind. – Inside there was no one to meet Deni as usual mistaken and completely ignored by everyone (good for him but he dont know it) so we have a

couple beers, ostensibly waiting, Deni outlines me
more facts & personal sophistries, there aint no one
coming, no friends, no enemies either, Deni is a per-
fect Taoist, nothing happens to him, the trouble runs
off his shoulders like water, as if he had pig grease
on em, he dont know how lucky he is, and here he's
got his boy at his side old Ti Jean who'll go anywhere
follow anyone for adventure. – Suddenly in the middle of the third or so beer he whoops and realizes we
missed the hourly Red Car train and that is going to
hold us up another hour in dismal Pedro, we want to
get to the glitters of Los Angeles if possible or Hollywood before all the bars closed, in my mind's eye I
see all the wonderful things Deni has planned for us
there and see, incomprehensible, unrememberable
what the images were I was now inventing ere we
got going and arrived at the actual scene, not the
screen but the dismal four-dimensional scene itself. –
Bang, Deni wants to take a cab and chase the Red
Car also with our beer cans in hand cartons we go
jogging down the street to a cab stand and hire one
to chase the Red Car, which the guy does without
comment, knowing the egocentricities of seamen
as a O how dismal cabdriver in a O how dismal

pierhead jumpin town. – Off we go – it's my suspicion he isnt really driving as fast as he ought to actually catch the Red Car, which hiballs right down that line, towards Compton and environs of LA, at 60 per. – My suspicion is he doesnt want to get a ticket and at the same time go fast enough to satisfy the whims of the seamen in the back – it's my suspicion he's just gonna gyp old Den out of a 5 dollar bill. – Nothing Den likes better than throw away his 5 dollar bills, too – he thrives on it, he lives for it, he all take voyages around the world working belowdecks among electrical equipment but worse than that take the abuse off officers and men (at four o'clock in the morning he's asleep in his bunk, 'Hey Carpenter, are you the carpenter or are you the chief bottlestopper or shithouse watcher, that goddam forward boom light is out again, I dont know who is using slingshots around here, and but I want that goddam light fixed we'll be pulling into Penang in 2 hours and goddam it if it's still dark at that time and I, and we dont got no light it's your ass not mine, see the chief about it') so Deni has to get up, and I can just see him do it, rub the innocent sleep from his eyes and wake to the cold howling world and wish he had a sword so he could cut the man's head off but at the same time he doesnt want to spend the rest of his life in a prison either, or get his own head partially cut off and spend the rest of his life paralyzed with a shoe brace in his neck and people bring him crap pans, so he crawls outa bed and does the bidding of every beast that has every yell to throw at him for every reason in the thousand and one electrical apparati on the goddam stinking steel jail which as far as I'm concerned, and floating on water too, is what they call a ship. – What is 5 dollars to a martyr? – 'Step on the gas, we gotta catch that car.'

'I'm going fast enough you'll get it.' He passes right through Cucamonga. 'At exactly 11:38 in 1947 or 1948, one, now I can't remember which one exactly, but I remember I done this for another seaman couple years ago and he passed right through –' and he goes on talking easing up so's not to pass through the insulting part of just barely beating a red light and I lay back in the seat and say:

'You coulda made that red light, we'll never make it now.'

'Listen Jack you wanta make it dontcha and not get fined by some traffic cop.'

'Where?' I say looking out the window and all
over the horizon at those marshes of night for signs
of a cop on a motorcycle or a cruiser – all you see is
marshes and great black distances of night and far
off, on hills, the little communities with Christmas
lights in their windows blearing red, blearing green,
blearing blue, suddenly sending pangs thru me and I
think, 'Ah America, so big, so sad, so black, you're
like the leafs of a dry summer that go crinkly ere
August found its end, you're hopeless, everyone you
look on you, there's nothing but the dry drear hope-
lessness, the knowledge of impending death, the
suffering of present life, lights of Christmas wont
save you or anybody, any more you could put Christmas lights on a dead bush in August, at night, and
make it look like something, what is this Christmas
you profess, in this void? . . . in this nebulous cloud?'

'That's perfectly alright' says Deni. 'Move right
along, we'll make it.' – He beats the next light to
make it look good but eases up for the next, and up
the track and back, you cant see any sign of the rear
or front of no Red Car, shoot – he comes to his place
where coupla years ago he'd dropped that seaman,
no Red Car, you can feel its absence, it's come and

gone, empty smell – you can tell by the electric still-
ness on the corner that something just was, & aint.

'Well I guess I missed it, goldang it,' says the cabdriver pushing his hat back to apologize and looking
real hypocritical about it, so Deni gives him five dollars and we get out and Deni says:

'Kerouac this means we have an hour to wait here
by the cold tracks, in the cold foggy night, for the
next train to LA.'

'That's okay' I say 'we got beer aint we, open one
up' and Deni fishes down for the old copper churchkey
and up comes two cans of beer spissing all over the
sad night and we up end the tin, and go slurp – two
cans each and we start throwing rocks at signs, dan-
cing around to keep warm, squatting, telling jokes,
remembering the past, Deni's going 'Hyra rrour
Hoo' and again I hear his great laugh ringing in the
American night and I try to tell him 'Deni the reason
I followed the ship all the way 3,200 miles from Staten
Island to goddam Pedro is not only because I wanta
get on and be seen going around the world and have
myself a ball in Port Swettenham and pick up on
gangee in Bombay and find the sleepers and the
fluteplayers in filthy Karachi and start revolutions of

27

my own in the Cairo Casbah and make it from Marseilles to the other side, but because of you, because, the things we used to do, where, I have a hell of a good time with you Den, there's no two ways about . . . I never have any money that I admit, I already owe you sixty for the bus fare, but you must admit I try . . . I'm sorry that I dont have any money ever, but you know I tried with you, that time . . . Well goddam, wa ahoo, shit, I want to get drunk tonight.' – And Deni says 'We dont have to hang around in the cold like this Jack, look there's a bar, over there' (a roadhouse gleaming redly in the misty night) 'it may be a Mexican Pachuco bar and we might get the hell beat out of us but let's go in there and wait the half hour we got with a few beers . . . and see if there's any cucamongas' so we head out there, across an empty lot. Deni is meanwhile very busy tellin me what a mess I've made of my life but I've heard that from everybody coast to coast and I dont care generally and I dont care tonight and this is my way of doing and saying things.

A coupla days later the SS *Roamer* sails away without me because they wouldnt let me get on at the union hall, I had no seniority, all I had to do they said was hang around a couple of months and work on the waterfront or something and wait for a coastwise ship to Seattle and I thought 'So if I'm gonna travel coasts I'm going to go down the coast I covet.' – So I see the *Roamer* slipping out of Pedro bay, at night again, the red port light and the green starboard light sneaking across the water with attendant ghostly following mast lights, vup! (the whistle of the little tug) – then the ever Gandharva-like, illusion-and-Maya-like dimlights of the portholes where some members of the crew are reading in bunks, others eating snacks in the crew mess, and others, like Deni, eagerly writing letters with a big red ink fountain pen assuring me that next time around the world I will get on the *Roamer*. – 'But I dont care, I'll go to Mexico' says I and walk off to the Pacific Red Car waving at Deni's ship vanishing out there . . .

Among the madcap pranks we'd pulled after that first night I told you about, we carried a huge tumbleweed up the gangplank at 3 A.M. Christmas Eve and shoved it into the engine crew fo'c'sle (where they were all snoring) and left it there. – When they woke up in the morning they thought they were somewhere else, in the jungle or something, and all went back to bed. – So when the Chief Engineer is yelling 'Who the hell put that tree on board!' (it was ten feet by ten feet, a big ball of dry twigs), way off across and down the ship's iron heart you hear Deni howling 'Hoo hoo hoo! *Who the hell put that tree on board!* Oh that Chief Engineer is a very funny m-a-h-n!'

# The Vanishing American Hobo

The American hobo has a hard time hoboing now-
adays due to the increase in police surveillance of
highways, railroad yards, sea shores, river bottoms,
embankments and the thousand-and-one hiding
holes of industrial night. – In California, the pack rat,
the original old type who goes walking from town
to town with supplies and bedding on his back, the
'Homeless Brother,' has practically vanished, along
with the ancient gold-panning desert rat who used
to walk with hope in his heart through struggling
Western towns that are now so prosperous they dont
want old bums any more. – 'Man dont want no pack
rats here even though they founded California' said
an old man hiding with a can of beans and an Indian
fire in a river bottom outside Riverside California in
1955. – Great sinister tax-paid police cars (1960 mod-
els with humorless searchlights) are likely to bear

down at any moment on the hobo in his idealistic lope to freedom and the hills of holy silence and holy privacy. – There's nothing nobler than to put up with a few inconveniences like snakes and dust for the sake of absolute freedom.

I myself was a hobo but only of sorts, as you see, because I knew someday my literary efforts would be rewarded by social protection – I was not a real hobo with no hope ever except that secret eternal hope you get sleeping in empty boxcars flying up the Salinas Valley in hot January sunshine full of Golden Eternity toward San Jose where mean-looking old bo's 'll look at you from surly lips and offer you something to eat and a drink too – down by the tracks or in the Guadaloupe Creekbottom.

The original hobo dream was best expressed in a lovely little poem mentioned by Dwight Goddard in his *Buddhist Bible*:

> Oh for this one rare occurrence
> Gladly would I give ten thousand pieces of gold!
> A hat is on my head, a bundle on my back,
> And my staff, the refreshing breeze and the full
>     moon.

In America there has always been (you will notice the peculiarly Whitmanesque tone of this poem, probably written by old Goddard) a definite special idea of footwalking freedom going back to the days of Jim Bridger and Johnny Appleseed and carried on today by a vanishing group of hardy old timers still seen sometimes waiting in a desert highway for a short bus ride into town for panhandling (or work) and grub, or wandering the Eastern part of the country hitting Salvation Armies and moving on from town to town and state to state toward the eventual doom of big-city skid rows when their feet give out. – Nevertheless not long ago in California I did see (deep in the gorge by a railroad track outside San Jose buried in eucalyptus leaves and the blessed oblivion of vines) a bunch of cardboard and jerrybuilt huts at evening in front of one of which sat an aged man puffing his 15¢ Granger tobacco in his corncob pipe (Japan's mountains are full of free huts and old men who cackle over root brews waiting for Supreme Enlightenment which is only obtainable through occasional complete solitude). In America camping is considered a healthy sport for Boy Scouts but a crime for mature men who have made it their vocation. – Poverty is considered a virtue among the monks of civilized nations – in America you spend a night in the calaboose if youre caught short without your vagrancy change (it was fifty cents last I heard of, Pard – what now?)

In Brueghel's time children danced around the hobo, he wore huge and raggy clothes and always looked straight ahead indifferent to the children, and the families didnt mind the children playing with the hobo, it was a natural thing. – But today mothers hold tight their children when the hobo passes through town because of what newspapers made the hobo to be – the rapist, the strangler, child-eater. – Stay away from strangers, they'll give you poison candy. Though the Brueghel hobo and the hobo today are the same, the children are different. – Where is even the Chaplinesque hobo? The old Divine Comedy hobo? The hobo is Virgil, he leadeth. – The hobo enters the child's world (like in the famous painting by Brueghel of a huge hobo solemnly passing through the washtub village being barked at and laughed at by children, St Pied Piper) but today it's an adult world, it's not a child's world. – Today the hobo's made to slink – everybody's watching the cop heroes on TV.

Benjamin Franklin was like a hobo in Pennsylvania; he walked through Philly with three big rolls under his arms and a Massachusetts halfpenny on his hat. – John Muir was a hobo who went off into the mountains with a pocketful of dried bread, which he soaked in creeks.

Did Whitman terrify the children of Louisiana when he walked the open road?

What about the Black Hobo? Moonshiner? Chicken snatcher? Remus? The black hobo in the South is the last of the Brueghel bums, children pay tribute and stand in awe making no comment. You see him coming out of the piney barren with an old unspeakable sack. Is he carrying coons? Is he carrying Br'er Rabbit? Nobody knows what he's carrying.

The Forty Niner, the ghost of the plains, Old Zacatecan Jack the Walking Saint, the prospector, the spirits and ghosts of hoboism are gone – but they (the prospectors) wanted to fill their unspeakable sacks with gold. – Teddy Roosevelt, political hobo – Vachel Lindsay, troubadour hobo, seedy hobo – how many pies for one of *his* poems? The hobo lives in a Disneyland, Pete-the-Tramp land, where everything is human lions, tin men, moondogs with rubber teeth, orange-and-purple paths, emerald castles in the distance looming, kind philosophers of witches. – No witch ever cooked a hobo. – The hobo has two watches you cant buy in Tiffany's, on one wrist the sun, on the other wrist the moon, both bands are made of sky.

> Hark! Hark! The dogs do bark,
> The beggars are coming to town;
> Some in rags, some in tags,
> And some in velvet gowns.

The Jet Age is crucifying the hobo because how can he hop a freight jet? Does Louella Parsons look kindly upon hobos, I wonder? Henry Miller would allow the hobos to swim in his swimming pool. – What about Shirley Temple, to whom the hobo gave the Bluebird? Are the young Temples bluebirdless?

Today the hobo has to hide, he has fewer places to hide, the cops are looking for him, *calling all cars, calling all cars, hobos seen in the vicinity of Bird-in-Hand* – Jean Valjean weighed with his sack of candelabra, screaming to youth, 'There's your *sou*, your *sou!*' Beethoven was a hobo who knelt and listened to the light, a deaf hobo who could not hear other hobo complaints. – Einstein the hobo with his ratty turtleneck sweater made of lamb, Bernard Baruch the disillusioned hobo sitting on a park bench with voice-catcher plastic in his ear waiting for John Henry, waiting for somebody very mad, waiting for the Persian epic. –

Sergei Esenin was a great hobo who took advantage of the Russian Revolution to rush around drinking potato juice in the backward villages of Russia (his most famous poem is called *Confessions of a Bum*) who said at the moment they were storming the Czar 'Right now I feel like pissing through the window at the moon.' It is the egoless hobo that will give birth to a child someday – Li Po was a mighty hobo. – Ego is the greatest hobo – Hail Hobo Ego! Whose monument someday will be a golden tin coffee can.

Jesus was a strange hobo who walked on water. –

Buddha was also a hobo who paid no attention to the other hobo. –

Chief Rain-In-The-Face, weirder even. –

W. C. Fields – his red nose explained the meaning of the triple world, Great Vehicle, Lesser Vehicle, Diamond Vehicle.

\*

The hobo is born of pride, having nothing to do with a community but with himself and other hobos and maybe a dog. – Hobos by the railroad embankments cook at night huge tin cans of coffee. – Proud was the way the hobo walked through a town by the back doors where pies were cooling on window sills, the hobo was a mental leper, he didnt need to beg to eat, strong Western bony mothers knew his tinkling beard and tattered toga, *come and get it*! But proud be proud, still there was some annoyance because sometimes when she called *come and get it*, hordes of hobos came, ten or twenty at a time, and it was kind of hard to feed that many, sometimes hobos were inconsiderate, but not always, but when they were, they no longer held their pride, they became bums – they migrated to the Bowery in New York, to Scollay Square in Boston, to Pratt Street in Baltimore, to Madison Street in Chicago, to 12th Street in Kansas City, to Larimer Street in Denver, to South Main Street in Los Angeles, to downtown Third Street in San Francisco, to Skid Road in Seattle ('blighted areas' all). –

The Bowery is the haven for hobos who came to the big city to make the big time by getting pushcarts and collecting cardboard. – Lots of Bowery bums are Scandinavian, lots of them bleed easily because they drink too much. – When winter comes bums drink a drink called smoke, it consists of wood alcohol and a drop of iodine and a scab of lemon, this they gulp down and wham! they hibernate all winter so as not to catch cold, because they dont live anywhere, and it gets very cold outside in the city in winter. – Sometimes hobos sleep arm-in-arm to keep warm, right on the sidewalk. Bowery Mission Veterans say that the beer-drinking bums are the most belligerent of the lot.

Fred Bunz is the great Howard Johnson's of the bums – it is located on 277 Bowery in New York. They write the menu in soap on the windows. – You see the bums reluctantly paying fifteen cents for pig brains, twenty-five cents for goulash, and shuffling out in thin cotton shirts in the cold November night to go and make the lunar Bowery with a smash of broken bottle in an alley where they stand against a wall like naughty boys. – Some of them wear adventurous rainy hats picked up by the track in Hugo Colorado or blasted shoes kicked off by Indians in the dumps of Juarez, or coats from the lugubrious salon of the seal and fish. – Bum hotels are white and tiled and seem as though they were upright johns. – Used to be bums told tourists that they once were successful doctors, now they tell tourists they were once guides for movie stars or directors in Africa and that when TV came into being they lost their safari rights.

In Holland they dont allow bums, the same maybe in Copenhagen. But in Paris you can be a bum – in Paris bums are treated with great respect and are rarely refused a few francs. – There are various kinds of classes of bums in Paris, the high-class bum has a dog and a baby carriage in which he keeps all his belongings, and that usually consists of old *France-Soirs*, rags, tin cans, empty bottles, broken dolls. – This bum sometimes has a mistress who follows him and his dog and carriage around. – The lower bums dont own a thing, they just sit on the banks of the Seine picking their nose at the Eiffel Tower. –

The bums in England have English accents, and it makes them seem strange – they dont understand bums in Germany. – America is the motherland of bumdom. –

American hobo Lou Jenkins from Allentown

Pennsylvania was interviewed at Fred Bunz's on the Bowery. – 'What you wanta know all this info for, what you want?'

'I understand that you've been a hobo travelin' around the country.'

'How about givin' a fella few bits for some wine before we talk.'

'Al, go get the wine.'

'Where's this gonna be in, the *Daily News*?'

'No, in a book.'

'What are you young kids doing here, I mean where's the drink?'

'Al's gone to the liquor store. – You wanted Thunderbird, wasnt it?'

'Yair.'

Lou Jenkins then grew worse – 'How about a few bits for a flop tonight?'

'Okay, we just wanta ask you a few questions like why did you leave Allentown?'

'My wife. – My wife. – Never get married. You'll never live it down. You mean to say it's gonna be in a book hey what I'm sayin'?'

'Come on say something about bums or something.' –

'Well whattaya wanta know about bums? Lot of 'em around, kinda tough these days, no money – lissen, how about a good meal?'

'See you in the Sagamore.' (Respectable bums' cafeteria at Third and Cooper Union.)

'Okay kid, thanks a lot.' – He opens the Thunderbird bottle with one expert flip of the plastic seal. – Glub, as the moon rises resplendent as a rose he swallows with big ugly lips thirsty to gulp the throat down, Sclup! and down goes the drink and his eyes be-pop themselves and he licks tongue on top lip and says 'H-a-h!' And he shouts 'Dont forget my name is spelled Jenkins, J-e-n-k-y-n-s.' –

Another character – 'You say that your name is Ephram Freece of Pawling New York?'

'Well, no, my name is James Russell Hubbard.'

'You look pretty respectable for a bum.'

'My grandfather was a Kentucky colonel.'

'Oh?'

'Yes.'

'Whatever made you come here to Third Avenue?'

'I really cant do it, I dont care, I cant be bothered, I feel nothing, I dont care any more. I'm sorry but –

42

somebody stole my razor blade last night, if you can lay some money on me I'll buy myself a Schick razor.'

'Where will you plug it in? Do you have such facilities?'

'A Schick injector.'

'Oh.'

'And I always carry this book with me – *The Rules of St Benedict*. A dreary book, but well I got another book in my pack. A dreary book too I guess.'

'Why do you read it then?'

'Because I found it – I found it in Bristol last year.'

'What are you interested in? You like interested in something?'

'Well, this other book I got there is er, yee, er, a big strange book – you shouldnt be interviewing me. Talk to that old nigra fella over there with the harmonica – I'm no good for nothing, all I want is to be left alone –'

'I see you smoke a pipe.'

'Yeah – Granger tobacco. Want some?'

'Will you show me the book?'

'No I aint got it with me, I only got this with me.' – He points to his pipe and tobacco.

43

'Can you say something?'

'Lightin flash.'

The American Hobo is on the way out as long as sheriffs operate with as Louis-Ferdinand Céline said, 'One line of crime and nine of boredom,' because having nothing to do in the middle of the night with everybody gone to sleep they pick on the first human being they see walking. – They pick on lovers on the beach even. They just dont know what to do with themselves in those five-thousand-dollar police cars with the two-way Dick Tracy radios except pick on anything that moves in the night and in the daytime on anything that seems to be moving independently of gasoline, power, Army or police. – I myself was a hobo but I had to give it up around 1956 because of increasing television stories about the abominable-ness of strangers with packs passing through by themselves independently – I was surrounded by three squad cars in Tucson Arizona at 2 A.M. as I was walking pack-on-back for a night's sweet sleep in the red moon desert:

'Where you goin'?'

'Sleep.'

'Sleep where?'

'On the sand.'

'Why?'

'Got my sleeping bag.'

'Why?'

'Studyin' the great outdoors.'

'Who are you? Let's see your identification.'

'I just spent a summer with the Forest Service.'

'Did you get paid?'

'Yeah.'

'Then why dont you go to a hotel?'

'I like it better outdoors and it's free.'

'Why?'

'Because I'm studying hobo.'

'What's so good about that?'

They wanted an *explanation* for my hoboing and came close to hauling me in but I was sincere with them and they ended up scratching their heads and saying 'Go ahead if that's what you want.' – They didnt offer me a ride four miles out to the desert.

And the sheriff of Cochise allowed me to sleep on the cold clay outside Bowie Arizona only because he didnt know about it. –

There's something strange going on, you cant even be alone any more in the primitive wilderness ('primitive areas' so-called), there's always a helicopter comes and snoops around, you need camouflage. – Then they begin to demand that you observe strange aircraft for Civil Defense as though you knew the difference between regular strange aircraft and any kind of strange aircraft. – As far as I'm concerned the only thing to do is sit in a room and get drunk and give up your hoboing and your camping ambitions because there aint a sheriff or fire warden in any of the new fifty states who will let you cook a little meal over some burning sticks in the tule brake or the hidden valley or anyplace any more because he has nothing to do but pick on what he sees out there on the landscape moving independently of the gasoline power army police station. – I have no ax to grind: I'm simply going to another world.

Ray Rademacher, a fellow staying at the Mission in the Bowery, said recently, 'I wish things was like they was when my father was known as Johnny the Walker of the White Mountains. – He once straightened out a young boy's bones after an accident, for a meal, and left. The French people around there called him *"Le Passant."'* (He who passes through.)

The hobos of America who can still travel in a

healthy way are still in good shape, they can go hide in cemeteries and drink wine under cemetery groves of trees and micturate and sleep on cardboards and smash bottles on the tombstones and not care and not be scared of the dead but serious and humorous in the cop-avoiding night and even amused and leave litters of their picnic between the grizzled slabs of Imagined Death, cussing what they think are real days, but Oh the poor bum of the skid row! There he sleeps in the doorway, back to wall, head down, with his right hand palm-up as if to receive from the night, the other hand hanging, strong, firm, like Joe Louis hands, pathetic, made tragic by unavoidable circumstance – the hand like a beggar's upheld with the fingers forming a suggestion of what he deserves and desires to receive, shaping the alms, thumb almost touching finger tips, as though on the tip of the tongue he's about to say in sleep and with that gesture what he couldnt say awake: 'Why have you taken this away from me, that I cant draw my breath in the peace and sweetness of my own bed but here in these dull and nameless rags on this humbling stoop I have to sit waiting for the wheels of the city to roll,' and further, 'I dont want to show my hand

47

but in sleep I'm helpless to straighten it, yet take this opportunity to see my plea, I'm alone, I'm sick, I'm dying – see my hand up-tipped, learn the secret of my human heart, give me the thing, give me your hand, take me to the emerald mountains beyond the city, take me to the safe place, be kind, be nice, smile – I'm too tired now of everything else, I've had enough, I give up, I quit, I want to go home, take me home O brother in the night – take me home, lock me in safe, take me to where all is peace and amity, to the family of life, my mother, my father, my sister, my wife and you my brother and you my friend – but no hope, no hope, no hope, I wake up and I'd give a million dollars to be in my own bed – O Lord save me –' In evil roads behind gas tanks where murderous dogs snarl from behind wire fences cruisers suddenly leap out like getaway cars but from a crime more secret, more baneful than words can tell.

The woods are full of wardens.